© Cedric Kim. All rights reserved. This book was written and published in 2019. Well, enjoy the book!

Table of Contents

Introduction (p3)

Forgetting about disability (p4)

There is no 'normal' (p7)

Why excluding people makes no sense (p9)

Unpopular opinions (p11)

Reputation based on stereotypes (p13)

Bullying (p14)

Making a difference (p15)

Why I wrote this book (p16)

Your notes (p17)

Introduction

This book is about the differences that make us all special, erasing the lines splitting society, and why there are no 'outsiders'.

This book is about being unique. This book is about how everyone has great potential.

Okay, enough introduction stuff, let's get to the main part of the book!

Forgetting about disability

Often, we associate having a disability with experiencing many hard situations on a day-to-day basis. Sure, in a way, this is correct. But many people with disabilities live surprisingly 'normal' lives.

Also, 'disability' is a very misleading word, as it suggests that people with disabilities are somehow unable to live normal lives.

Many people will mentally exaggerate another person's disability, leading to exclusion, bullying, and in the end, more social issues than issues that are actually caused by a disability.

Nowadays, there is more bullying against disabled people than ever before. This bullying should not be accepted, in fact, no bullying should ever be accepted.

By drawing a line between 'disabled' and 'normal' people, we are splitting up society into two groups, with many stereotypes being thrown around.

Our differences are what make us all unique, and one of the only reasons to live. Disabled people don't have such a severity in being different that they should be separated from the rest of the world.

Imagine if there were no disabled people, and no other people to replace them. Now, imagine if this was done because these people were disabled. We would have wiped out about 15% of the whole population due to stereotypes. That doesn't sound good, right?

There is no 'normal'

I mentioned the word 'normal' several times in the last chapter, and always with quotes around it. Why? Because I believe that there is no 'normal'.

Everyone is different in one way or another. Need proof? Come up with a few ways that you're unique and see how much time it takes.

Are you back? Good. Now, you might be thinking: Yeah, I'm kind of unique, but so is everyone else. There must be some kind of 'just unique' and 'truly unique', right?

It didn't make sense to me at first, either. I mean, if everyone is unique, what's the point? There's your 'normal'. HA! The end!

Are you still there? Yes, I was joking. There are no different levels of unique, everyone's 'uniqueness' has an equal potential to start a breakthrough.

We're all unique, and we all have huge potential, and that's the only thing that will ever be the same.

Why excluding people makes absolutely no sense

Being excluded from a group is a very harsh feeling to many people and being an 'outsider' can be a horrible feeling, especially when a person's friend is in a group without that person.

Excluding people from a group often doesn't make sense. Often, this is because of stereotypes similar or exactly like the ones in the first chapter of this book.

Sometimes the reason is harsher, like because someone has a different gender, race, age, or even where they come from.

For example, several elderly people have been fired from several different companies due to their age.

Groups of people with a certain race have been highly discriminated against, however, because this specific racial discrimination topic is such a sensitive topic, we will not be discussing it any further in this book.

Unpopular opinions

Nowadays, having an unpopular opinion can result in ruining your reputation and being subject to more bullying than ever before.

This has led many people to avoid sharing unpopular opinions (especially online), in fear of being considered an 'outsider' from the 'normal'.

When people see that many other people are doing something as opposed to something else, they do the same. This means that people are changing their opinions to fit in with other people, who are doing the exact same thing.

But where does it start? It usually starts with people who are actually stating their opinions. When more people are on one side than the other, people start 'agreeing' with the more popular opinion. But, again, this is only to fit in. Many people feel that it's important to fit in, but this is what ruins the differences that make everyone unique.

Reputation based on stereotypes

Your reputation can be seriously affected by stereotypes on your beliefs. Having an unpopular opinion can destroy your reputation.

But why? There are many stereotypes around many unpopular opinions, involving that you shouldn't trust some people based on their beliefs. This, of course, is not true in any way, but many people think this way.

Reputation should not be based on stereotypes, but it's almost unavoidable in modern society, with many stereotypes being spread without much thought.

Bullying

Bullying can seriously hurt a person's feelings and make them feel left out from the group of 'normal' people.

Bullying is a serious topic and in the modern day, bullying happens at large scales via the internet.

This leaves people more sensitive than ever before about what they choose to believe, in fear of being bullied based on stereotypes.

Making a difference

How can you make a difference? How can you change things? How can you help solve the problems discussed in this book. It can be as simple as a social media post to spread awareness. Or standing up to bullies and spreading words of kindness.

You can change things. You can make it happen. This is just the beginning.

#YouAreNotAnOutsider

Why I wrote this book

I wrote this book because I've felt like an outsider several times and have gained lots of information on the topic. I decided that I wanted to write a book about it.

I started spending hours of my free time writing this book. I understand that it's quite short, but I'm just getting started with writing.

I wanted to inspire people with this book, to inspire people to make a difference and change things.

Your notes

If you own this copy of this book, then I highly recommend that you mark it up in some way to take notes. In this section of this book, you can write longer notes and keep them with you in this book.

Lightning Source UK Ltd.
Milton Keynes UK
UKHW051809230223
417331UK00008B/38